MAPPA MUNDI

THE MAP OF THE WORLD AT HEREFORD CATHEDRAL

A brief guide by

MERYL JANCEY

NEW EDITION

Published by
Hereford Cathedral Enterprises for
The Dean and Chapter of Hereford.
1995

ISBN 0 904642 06 2

Photographs by Gordon Taylor

First Edition 1987

Acknowledgements

I owe a great debt of gratitude for the help I have received in preparing this booklet from Mr R. Boulton in designing the work and Miss P. E. Morgan for saving me from many errors. Any that remain are my responsibility.

E.M.J.

DATE

MAP OF THE WORLD

The map of the world, newly displayed at Hereford Cathedral, was probably made within the last ten years of the thirteenth century. Its style, general appearance and handwriting make it unlikely that it was written later than that, while internal evidence of its content suggests that it cannot be earlier. The Snowdonian towns of Conway and Caernarvon are shown with a prominence only to be expected after Edward I's conquest of Wales and the building of the castles which were a marvel to their times.[1]

THE MAP AT HEREFORD

We have no knowledge of how or why or when this map came to Hereford. The first reference to it occurs about 1682, the date of the compilation of the book *History from marble* by Thomas Dingley who had spent some time in Herefordshire examining its antiquities.[2] Among his descriptions of the monuments and memorials in the cathedral he mentions the presence there of an old map on vellum, written by a monk. The implication is that the map had been there for some time.

The idea of maps as illustrations, particularly in bible studies, would not have been new in the age from which this map speaks to us. References to maps of the world in catalogues of medieval libraries are not uncommon,[3] and more maps have survived from the twelfth and early thirteenth century to show that a real tradition in map-making was in existence.[4] The large wall maps like this one at Hereford were the product of the thirteenth century. They would have appealed to the then current passion for organising knowledge in encyclopedic form and are a further example of the intellectual preoccupations of that age. We know, from surviving fragments, that such maps were made, probably in some quantity, but the Hereford example is the only one known to have survived in its entirety.[5]

It is drawn on a large piece of vellum (prepared calf-skin), measuring 64 by 54 inches. Now somewhat dulled by the passage of time, the brilliant colours and rich decoration have faded, but traces enough remain to show that this must have been made in a well-found workshop in which a skilled draughtsman would have access to all he needed. Its making would have been an expensive business.

Most of the space is taken up with a picture of the habitable world drawn within a circle and shown essentially as an island. That the form is circular does not

(1) For a discussion of the dating, see the memoir by G. R. Crone, accompanying *Reproductions of early manuscript maps*, III, *The World Map of Richard of Haldingham . . .*, Royal Geographical Society, 1954.

(2) Camden Society, Old series, 94, 97.

(3) Lincoln, for example, had such a map. It must have been in volume form, for it is listed alongside books located in a cupboard. R.M. Woolley, *Catalogue of manuscripts in Lincoln Cathedral Chapter library*, 1927.

(4) Bagrow, ed. by Skelton, *History of cartography*, London, 1964. Bevan and Phillott, *Medieval geography, an essay in illustration of the Hereford Mappa Mundi*, London and Hereford, 1874.

(5) British Library leaflet, issued 1987, to accompany an exhibition of ancient maps, entitled *Lost Worlds*. A similar, though even larger map was formerly at Ebstorf in West Germany. It was destroyed in the 1939-45 war. A lithograph reproduction is in Hereford Cathedral where it can be compared with the Hereford Map.

mean that men of the thirteen century necessarily thought of the world as round. The map here follows a cartographical tradition, a convention, derived from Roman times in which the habitable world was drawn within a diagrammatic scheme. This was a circle, bisected by the letter T, the strokes of which roughly represented the rivers and seas dividing the three land masses of Asia, Europe and Africa. In such maps, the east was usually given at the top.

JERUSALEM AT THE CENTRE

This convention easily accommodated the Christian interpretation, in literal terms, concerning the position of Jerusalem as the centre of the habitable world.[6] By identifying Jerusalem at the centre and recognising the east at the top, we can see that this map roughly follows these conventions. They have led to distortions in the shapes and relative sizes of the land masses, but even so, one of the main purposes of a map is fulfilled. Places are shown in relation to one another.

ASIA AFRICA EUROPE

The whole of the top half is occupied by Asia which includes the far north-east and India and stretches not only to the near east and Arabia but Egypt as well. The bottom half is divided into two, Europe to the left, Africa to the right. Unfortunately, a mistake here throws us once more into confusion. Europe and Africa are wrongly labelled. Europe to the left is given as Africa, and Africa to the right, as Europe.

A mistake like this is of the kind arising in copying or adapting from another version. It is not the only one of its type. Taken together, these errors lend substance to the theory that this map is a late example in a school of fashion for such maps, and that it is directly dependent on an earlier version belonging to an established tradition which itself perpetuated errors. An accomplished scribe was working within that tradition without always fully understanding his material.

The form of the map is then derivative, following medieval tradition drawn from ancient classical conventions. Its geographical content is equally derivative, based to a great degree on classical learning to which little addition has been made. Its historical material is drawn from a large variety of sources, including the Bible. Information about travels and natural history, often at second, third or fourth hand, originates in classical writings. A true product of its age, the map seems to claim authenticity by demonstrating awareness of ancient authority rather than by illustrating scientific knowledge based on actual experience. It provides, in terms of a map, an illustrated compendium, a 'summa', of current knowledge.

Something of its purpose can be better understood by the drawings and comment filling the spaces between the rim of the circle confining the world and

(6) To place Jerusalem in the centre was to give a literal interpretation to passages in the Bible, particularly Ezekiel, V, 5, 'This is Jerusalem: I have set her in the midst of the nations . . . round about her'.

the border of the skin. In these, it would seem that the scribe/draughtsman has stepped outside the framework of his model and made his own editorial complement to the text. He gives us the title of the map, explains its authority, tells us his name, and indicates its overall theme.

TITLE

The title is written rather small above the head of the horseman in the bottom right hand corner. Here, we are told, is an illustration of the description of the world given by Orosius.[7] He lived in the fifth century, was a pupil of St. Augustine and wrote a great work to confute the pagans, of which the seventh book gave a description of the world. This work was well-known,[8] and was much used by others so that references to it may be to writings at several removes from his book. What matters here is that the world map is meant to be seen as an illustration of a written description or account.

AUTHOR

In the bottom left-hand corner we are given the map's authority. A drawing shows Caesar Augustus wearing a papal tiara,[9] issuing his mandate, authenticated with a fine vesica-shaped seal, to commissioners named Nicodoxus, Theoclitus and Polyclitus, to make a survey or description of the world. There is a confusion of stories here, one that Julius Caesar appointed these three commissioners for this purpose, and the other that Caesar Augustus ordered such a survey. This is the one connected with the reference in St. Luke's Gospel, where the words 'to be taxed' have been given as the English translation of the Latin word describeretur. The survey ordered by Caesar Augustus did bear fruit in further commentaries which were known to Pliny, and it is from Pliny that much of the learning displayed in the map is ultimately derived.

Below this drawing, in the bottom left-hand corner, we are given the name of the man who made and drew the map. Enough has been said to suggest that 'made' cannot mean created, thought up, from new. It rather signifies the crafting of the work by a master draughtsman who was also a skilled scribe, able to copy handwriting as well as draw and paint. He has written a message, asking all who have this 'estoire', or shall hear or see or read it, to pray to Jesus for pity on Richard of Haldingham and Lafford who has made and drawn it, that joy in heaven be given him. Haldingham and Lafford are old forms of the names Holdingham and Sleaford in Lincolnshire. This Richard has, in time past, been

(7) *Descriptio Orosii de Ornesta [Ormesta] Mundi Sicut Interius Ostenditur*
Orosius' work was sometimes referred to in an abbreviated form as ORMESTA (Orosius' History of the World). There would be no need to use this form when Orosius' name is given in full. It suggests a lack of understanding of the shortened title.

(8) King Alfred had commissioned its translation into Anglo-Saxon though that version would, of course, have been virtually forgotten in the thirteenth century.

(9) Caesar Augustus was venerated in the Middle Ages because of a legend that he had been favoured with a vision of the Blessed Virgin and the newborn Christ. This story is told in the *Golden Legend*, a collection of lives of the saints and other material conducive to piety compiled in the mid-thirteenth century, and extremely popular in the following centuries.

equated with one Richard de Bello, known to have been prebendary of Holdingham and Sleaford in the cathedral of Lincoln in the years 1276-1283.[10]

The map was, however, not made as a leisure activity of a learned cleric taking time off from other duties. Richard was the maker in the sense of patron, of a work carried out by possibly a team of professionals producing a composite statement about the world directed to an educated but not necessarily learned society.

We are told exactly what the map was intended to be. It is called an 'estoire' a word which carried connotations of both 'story' and 'description', and 'story' used in the sense of giving information alongside its associations. This is what the map so magnificently does. Take into the mind any word — Crete for example — and there it is, on the map, complete with labyrinth.

THEME

Above the round picture of the habitable world, at the very apex of the map, we are given a drawing of Christ in Majesty, sitting in judgement. The blessed move to Paradise, the wicked are dragged to Hell.

The world lying under this judgement is shown as the work of God's Creation and the scene of man's history and redemption.[11] Here we have the map's theme. It is identical with that of the great west portals of Gothic cathedrals, but worked out in terms of a map.[12] Again, he has chosen to use Norman-French for the words spoken by the Blessed Virgin and for the angels' trumpet blasts.

THE TRAVELLER

In the bottom right-hand corner is a lively drawing of a huntsman with a brace of greyhounds, giving what appears to be a parting salutation to a rider on horseback who looks back with a wave of his hand to the great round world above his head. It would be agreeable to see this as an indication that having studied the map, we can go our way, having had guidance for our travels. 'Passe-Avant' cries the huntsman; 'go forward'. If we do so, and study the map in greater detail, we shall be guided not so much in space as in time, to the age which produced it and for which it now serves as a great interpreter.

(10) If the prebendary is the man it is very strange that he does not give his title as *Magister,* and describe his prebend as in the cathedral of *Lincoln,* the usual manner of describing such status. He could not, in any case have described himself so after 1283, and this is a very early date for the completion of the map. For the career of Richard de Bello, and also for Richard de Bello II, who became a prebendary of Norton in Hereford cathedral in 1305, see Emden, *A Biographical register of the University of Oxford to A.D. 1500,* vol I, Oxford, 1957. Sometimes the two men have been taken as one, but this is unlikely.

(11) This is why, if the antiquary Richard Gough, in his *British Topography* (1780), is correct, the map could have been used as an altar piece, reverenced as such during the middle ages and then hidden away at the Reformation. Recent work on the re-discovered panels once used as framing the map strongly support this theory. See *"The Mappa Mundi triptych",* by Martin Bailey in Apollo, Vol 137, no 376, June 1993.

(12) Emile Male, *The Gothic image,* Ikon Edition, 1972, and especially chapter VI.

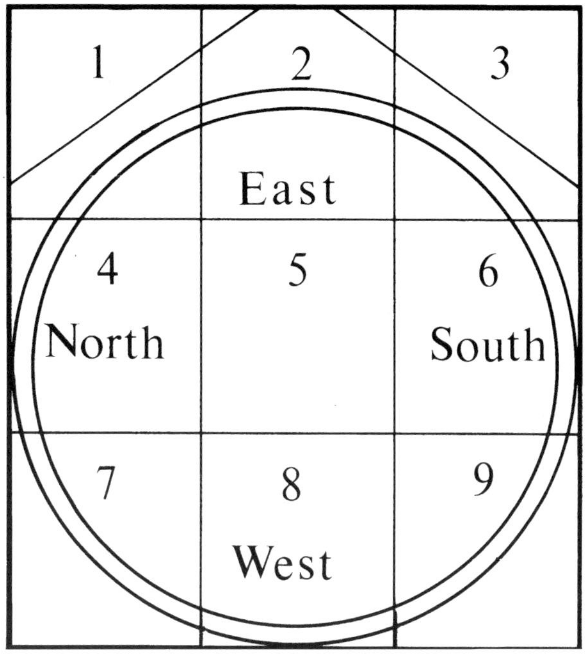

The map has been divided into 9 sections, as shown in the diagram, each section accompanied by a description. This arrangement has ensured that all the illustrations, except the first which shows the whole map, are to the same scale.

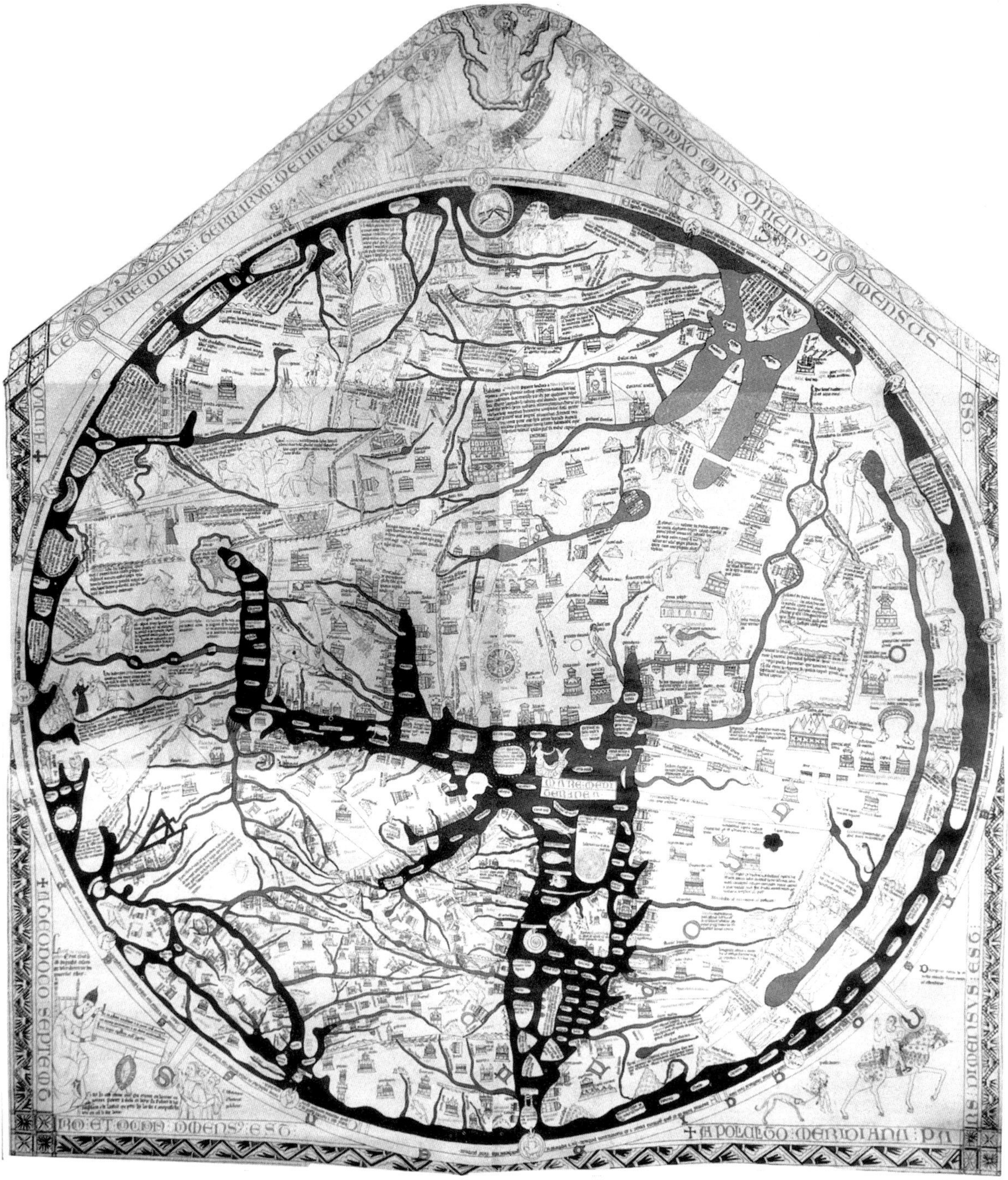

THE ROUND WORLD

The whole work has a patterned border, part of which is a conventional design, and part a rather dull drawing of a twining plant. The spaces between the border and the diagram of the world are filled with drawings, the Last Judgement at the top. A frieze records Julius Caesar's commissioning of a survey of the world.

THE CIRCLES

The habitable world is drawn within two circles, the outer divided into the four quarters, the east at the top, the inner giving a table of the winds. The nature of each is noted (Auster, for example, one of the south winds, is hot and humid and brings forth flowers), and each is illustrated either by a grotesque figure or by a breath-exhaling beast. Looped to the inner circle are gold letters spelling out round the map the word MORS, apparently signifying that man and his world shall pass away.

MAIN FEATURES

The Holy Land takes up the centre of the map. The Mediterranean Sea stretches to the west, to the Pillars of Hercules (the straits of Gibralter), at the bottom. The Red Sea and the Persian Gulf, painted scarlet, lie south of east, and merge with the Indian ocean. The British Isles lie to the north west. To the south, a long blue ribbon represents the upper reaches of the river Nile. The course of this river remained a mystery until the last century. Here we have the theory that it flowed out of Africa and then submerged to rise again to pass through Egypt and so, by its delta, into the southern Mediterranean.

SYMBOLS AND CONTENT

Most of the writing and the drawings are made in very black ink. Rivers are painted blue. Some of the seas may once have been green, but have now faded to sepia. Gold and vermilion have been used to pick out detail. Mountain ranges are mostly indicated by conventional scalloped designs, towns and cities by walls and towers.

Superimposed on the basic geographical content are drawings, usually accompanied by descriptions, illustrating man's history and the marvels of the natural world. These supply a compilation of knowledge current in the thirteenth century. The map form must have been given it a new dimension by showing something of the relation to each other of places familiar from many sources and the location of their associated wonders, both past and present.

Section 1

SECTION 1.

A small part of the scene of the Last Judgement appears at the top of this section of the map. At the angel's trumpet blast the dead burst from their graves.

Within the circle of the world, the far north-eastern regions are depicted in terms indicating a kind of horror at the cold and desolation found in them. The outer seas are dotted with islands with strange inhabitants. One race, the Phanesii, is shown with their great ears used as wrappings. Another has the hooves of horses for feet.

Opposite the island of the bat-eared people is a text concerning the Seres, the Chinese, the inhabitants coming first after the desert regions, who make clothes from silk.[1]

A blunt peninsular shape alongside the coast is filled with a long, and rather garbled, account concerning the imprisonment (by Alexander) of the sons of Cain. They will break out in the days of Anti-Christ.

To the right of the lands of China, the source of the river Oxus is given, just below the city of Samarkand, and to the right of this river, what would otherwise have been a blank space is filled with two drawings, one of a monstrous bird-headed creature[2] and the other of the pelican feeding her brood with the life-blood of her wounded breast.[3]

(1) In spite of constrictions caused by the conventional shape, the map here shows a particularly vivid imaginative grasp of these empty unknown regions. Nearly four hundred years later, Milton, using the stored learning of the culture to which he was heir, has written what describes it for us:

> As when a vulture on Imaus bred,
> Whose snowy ridge the roving Tartar bounds,
> Dislodging from a region scarce of prey
> To gorge the flesh of lambs or yeanling kids
> On hills where flocks are fed, flies toward the springs
> Of Ganges or Hydaspes, Indian streams,
> But in his way lights on the barren plains
> Of Sericana, where Chineses drive
> With sails and wind their cany waggons light.
> So on this windy land the Fiend . . .

(2) This race of monsters would appear to be confused with a people described by Pliny, the Cicones.

(3) There does not seem to be any particular reason for putting the pelican here, except that there was room for it. The legend of the pelican's habit of feeding her young by wounding her own breast arose from a misinterpretation of observation — she plucks her breast down for nesting material. She became, to the medieval mind, a type of Christ's love, and appears over and over again. A fine roof-boss in the Bishop's cloisters, Hereford Cathedral, is one such depiction.

Section 2

SECTION 2

At the apex of the map, the figure of Christ in Majesty sits at the Day of Judgement among clouds of glory. To His Right, an angel with a trumpet summons the blessed to joy, to His Left, another pronounces doom to the lost. The Blessed Virgin pleads for pity on those who have shown devotion to her.[1]

Immediately beneath, within the circles defining the world, The Terrestrial Paradise is drawn as an island walled with flame. Adam and Eve are engaged in eating the forbidden fruit. Below the island and a little to the right, an angel brandishing a sword bars the way of return.

Spread below these scenes, in a wide swathe across the map we are given India. The river Ganges rising in mountains called Osca, flows east, bifurcated to form a triangle representing its delta. A long textual note describes India, referring to its size, its 5000 cities, the variety of its peoples, its wealth of precious stones and metals, the numbers of its beasts and serpents, all more easily read of than depicted. The map-maker does his best with this plenitude. The Sciapod shelters himself with his one large foot from the heat of the sun,[2] the Gangines delicately nourish themselves on their only food, the scent of apples. Legendary birds called Alerion rest among mountains, an alligator lurks on the banks of the Hydaspes,[3] a parrot perches on a rock.[4]

Much of the historical material refers to the stories of the Indian campaigns of Alexander the Great. The town of Bucephala is marked, founded on the site where his horse died after the Hydaspes battle (325 B.C.), and the altars shown which he set up before turning away from India.

Great rivers flow south, the Hydaspes, the Indus, and below them, the Tigris passing through the lands of Persia and Arabia. A little below this river, from a little tabernacle, a face looks out. It must be intended for Abraham, in Ur of the Chaldees.[5]

(1) The image of the Blessed Virgin as nursing mother was much loved from the thirteenth century onwards. Our Lord shows the wounds by which He redeemed the world, she pleads for sinners by the milk that nourished Him.

(2) Monoculi (one-eyed) is written in error for monocoli (one-legged).

(3) Most of the information about creatures of the east is ultimately derived from the writings of the elder Pliny. The alligator is, after all, almost as strange as the others.

(4) There is a blunder in the parrot's name. The form should be from *psitacus* not *spitacus*.

(5) The Lord summoned Abraham from Ur of the Chaldees on his great migration to the land of Canaan. Representation of him in a tabernacle may well be an example of the literal treatment of the biblical account of one of the Lord's appearances to Abraham while he was sitting at the door of his tent *(tabernacula)*, in the heat of the day. (Gen. XI. 28 and Gen. XVIII. 1). The accompanying Latin inscription makes so little sense that a copying mistake must be assumed.

Section 3

SECTION 3

At the top, the right hand part of the drawing of the Last Judgement shows the wicked being dragged to the devil and so passed on to the monster's jaws which are the mouth of Hell.[1]

Below, the world curves away, and we leave India to the east, suitably symbolised by its elephant complete with a castellated kind of howdah, illustrating the use of these animals in war.[2]

Rivers of India debouch into the scarlet-painted seas which combine to flow round the island of Ceylon. An inscription reads that the island has two summers, two winters and two springs and that it abounds in elephants and dragons. Portraits of dragon-like creatures are supplied. Other islands are shown in these seas, including Ophir, evocative of Eastern riches.[3]

The lower arm of the scarlet waters is the Red Sea, its shore to the south in the bottom of the picture forming the boundary of Nubia which is also washed by the outer sea which here contains an unidentified island called Ciprus. A note reads that the peoples of Nubia have Christian sympathies. The lower course of the Nile emerges to flow through the Nubian mountains from a source which carries the name Moses. This would appear to be a transfer of association with his rescue from the bulrushes.

(1) The representation of Hell mouth as the jaws of Leviathan arose from commentaries on the Book of Job. The theme is constantly depicted in many forms of art throughout the middle ages. Its treatment here is perhaps best compared with that in wall-paintings like the one over the chancel arch in the church of South Leigh, Oxfordshire.

(2) The drawing of the elephant illustrates an interesting and possibly highly significant point about his map. The animals and monsters are portrayed, alongside textual descriptions as evidence for them, as straight-forward factual depictions of creatures. They are not shown or described as allegories or 'types'. The elephant is here a beast of war, not a symbol of the innocence of Adam and Eve. The source behind the drawings is ancient natural history and mythology rather than Christian traditions of thinking of such creatures as symbols.

(3) There is little geographical reality here. It appears rather to be the grouping together by association of names signifying the fabled wealth of the east. 'And they came to Ophir and fetched from thence gold, four hundred and twenty talents', I Kings IX. 28. Ancient knowledge of the east and its exotic products would have come from sea-traders journeying along the coasts and was derived from narrative and heresay evidence of travellers. The day of navigational charts was yet to come.

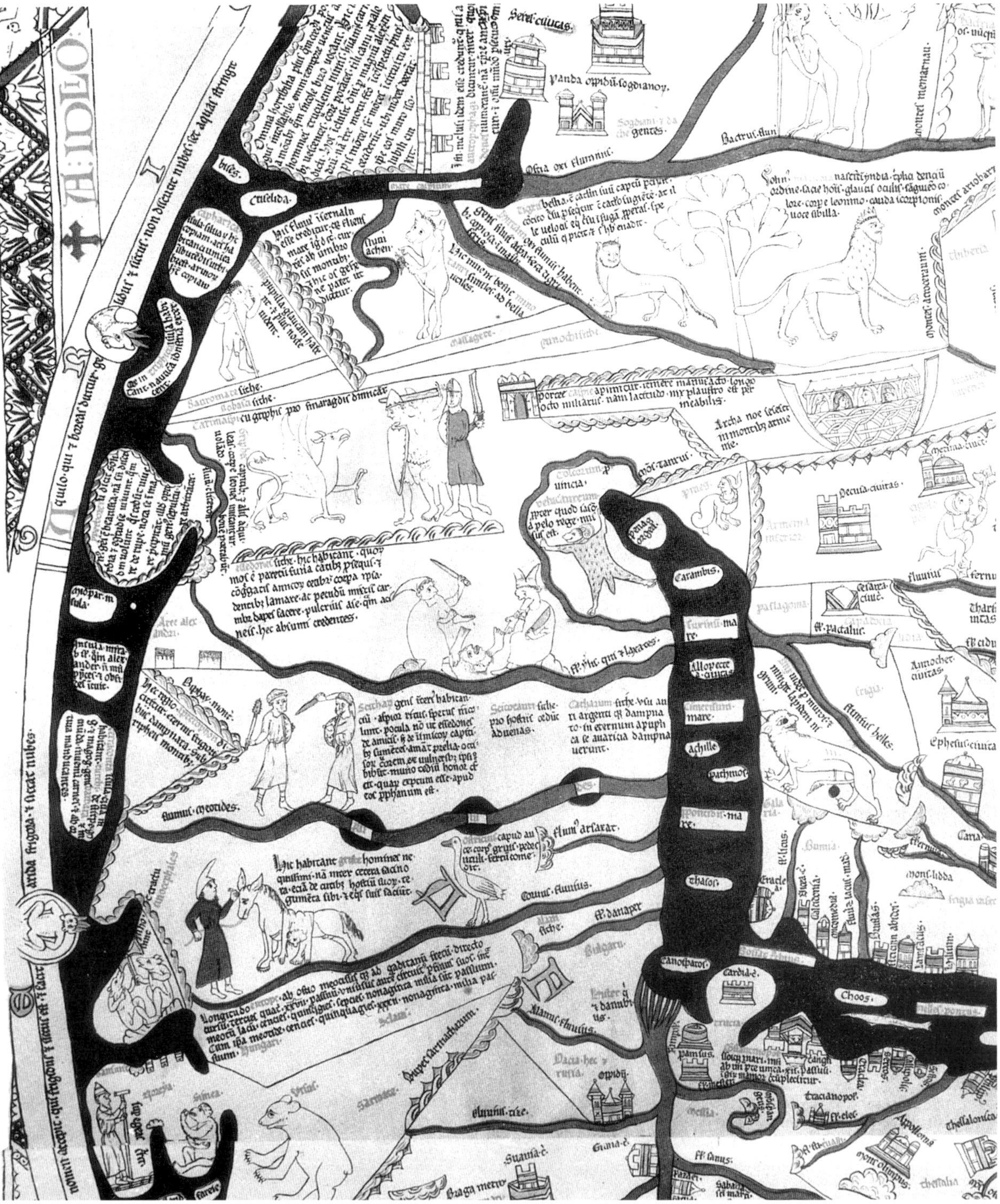

Section 4

SECTION 4

The middle part of this section is occupied by the Black Sea. The river Danube and its delta are shown at the bottom, flowing into it from the west. A little to the right is Constantinople.[1] To the right of the Black Sea is the northern part of Asia Minor, partly taken up with a drawing of the lynx.[2] Near the furthest point of the Black Sea is Colchis, with the Golden Fleece which Jason sought stretched out. A little above this, to the right, is Mount Taurus and above this again, the Caspian Gates, the narrow pass through the mountains beyond which lie the lands surrounding the Caspian sea. The mountain regions at the head of the Black Sea include those of Armenia among which Noah's ark has come to rest. The heads of birds and serpents can be seen through porthole-like openings alongside Noah and his family.

To the left of the Black Sea we are provided with many marvels, including the iron-eating ostrich, Scythians fighting, the Essedenes who eat the flesh of their dead parents, the emerald-guarding griffon and the grey-eyed race who see better by night than by day. Not far away is the Minotaur, bull-headed and gently holding his tail. To his right is the Hyrcanean tiger, famed for speed and ferocity.[3] In the regions depicted in the right hand corner we again approach India with its marvels, the fig tree and the manticora, a man-headed beast with the body of a lion. The text alongside refers to its scorpion tail, but the drawing does not show this.

The river Oxus flows into the Caspian sea,[4] which communicates with the encircling ocean. A promontory projecting into it carries a legend describing the blest state of the Hyperboreans who know not discord or sickness and when tired of life throw themselves into the sea. A little further down is the island of Terraconta inhabited by a race descended from Gog and Magog.[5] Another promontory is filled with dog-headed people. Near them are the Grifones who used the bodies of their enemies as horse-trappings.

It must be remembered that the form of the map has caused much constriction here, so that the peoples near the ocean of the far north are confusedly close to those of western and central Asia.

(1) Constantinople is drawn upside down, possibly to incorporate in the space the indication that it was surrounded on three sides by water.

(2) *The lynx sees through walls and produces a black stone.* This stone of congealed urine was fabled to have curative properties.

(3) The Hyrcanean tiger long remained a symbol of ferocity. v. *Macbeth*
'What man dare, I dare
Approach thou like the Rugged Russian bear
The arm'd rhinoceros or the Hyrcan tiger . . .'

(4) The Oxus was first discovered for the western world by Alexander the Great. It was thought then, and for long afterwards, that it entered the Caspian sea. It flows into the Aral, unknown to ancient geography.

(5) Gog and Magog have survived in a confusion of legends. Basic to them all is that they were of a monstrous brood and enemies of the Kingdom of God. These ideas probably originated in references in Ezekiel and Revelation.

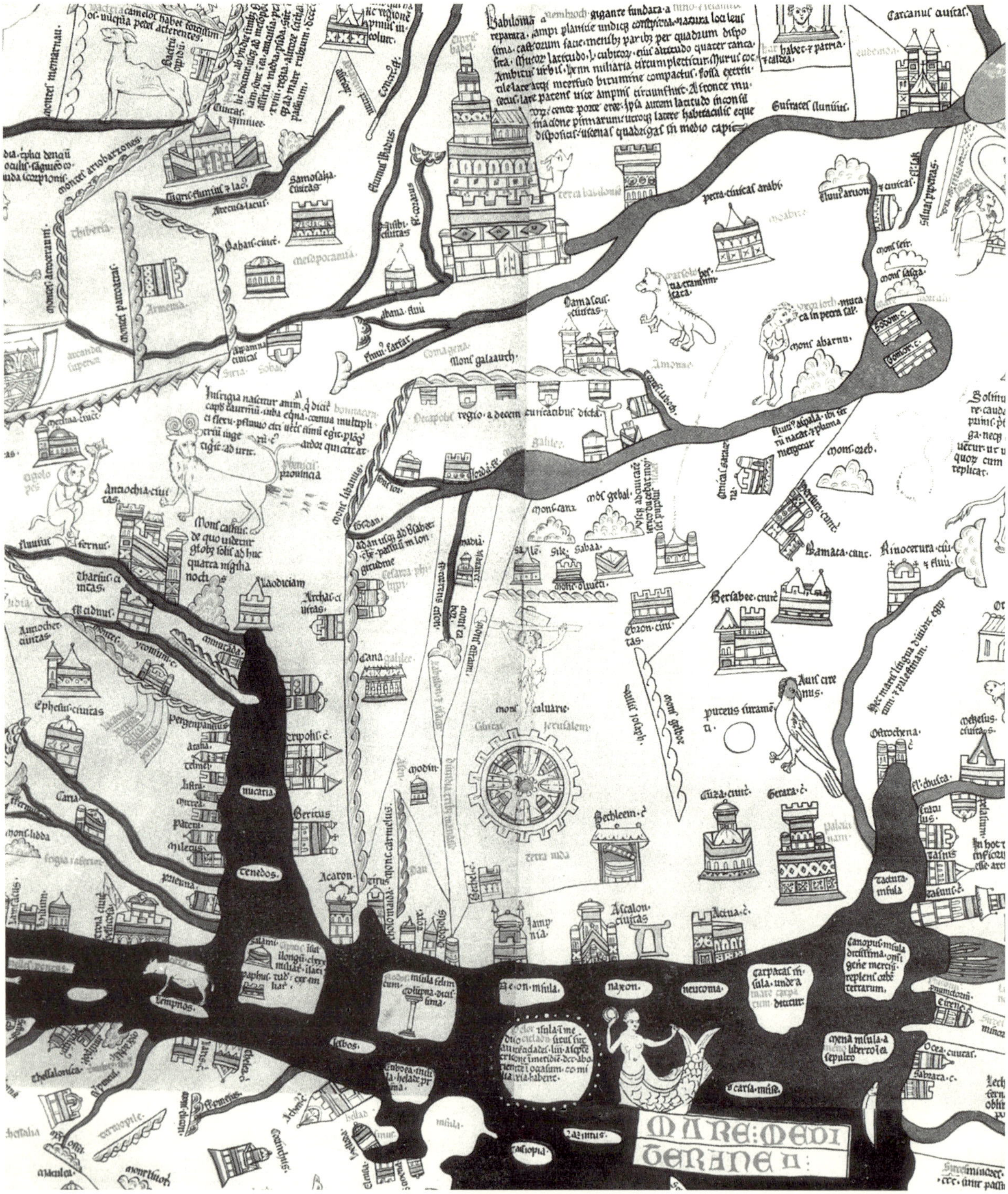

Section 5

SECTION 5

This is the central portion of the map. It contains the Holy Land, with Jerusalem shown as a large circular walled city. Above is Mount Calvary, with the Crucifixion and, a little beyond, the Mount of Olives. Bethlehem, with a stable, is rightly related to Jerusalem, to the south-west.

The map is here so filled with information that it is difficult to identify the geographical setting, partly because so disproportionate an amount of space is given to the biblical lands of the Old Testament that Asia Minor itself, to the left, is sadly cramped.

The Holy Land is washed by the eastern Mediterranean sea which is decorated with a large mermaid, and studded with islands. Among them Rhodes is clearly discerned from the drawing of the Colossus, shown as a column, one of the wonders of the ancient world. An arm of the Mediterranean thrusts eastwards into the land mass of Asia Minor. On its northern shore (to the left), the coast is lined with a number of towns, most of them easily identifiable from the *Acts of the Apostles*. Syrian Antioch is particularly impressive a little further east. Moving on from Antioch, we arrive at the regions of Armenia and Mesopotamia and the source of the river Tigris, passing on the way the Bonnacon,[1] and the Ugolopes.[2] Eastward again, and we are on the fringes of India in the top left corner, marked by the Bactrian camel.[3] The most prominent feature in the eastern or top half of this part of the map is the Tower of Bable. The long text near the drawing refers, however, not to the tower, but to Babylon. The river near these features is the Euphrates, flowing towards the Red Sea, through Arabia and past Petra. Slightly below the river is Damascus, rather oddly placed in relation to other features. We then return to the Holy Land proper, and can identify the river Jordan rising in Mount Libanus and flowing through the Sea of Galilee to the Dead Sea where Sodom and Gomorrah lie submerged, and Lot's wife stands looking sadly back at them. Below and a little to the right of the sea of Galilee, Jericho is marked with the legend that Moses led the people of Israel to the city of Jericho. Here ends the track of the wanderings of the Israelites.[4]

Returning to the sea again, we arrive at the northern shore of Africa and the lighthouse of Alexandria.[5]

(1) The Bonnacon is described as having a bull's head, a horse's mane, and curling horns. When chased it discharges dung over three acres and this burns whatever it touches.

(2) The Ugolopes, who have webbed feet and a tail, have not been identified.

(3) The Bactrian camel is correctly shown with two humps. It carries the note that these camels do not wear out their hooves.

(4) The Latinity here is another example of rather strange copying by a scribe whose Latin cannot be relied on. He has written *usque ad civitatem Jerico ducebat Moyses pupolus (sic) Israel.*

(5) See Section 6.

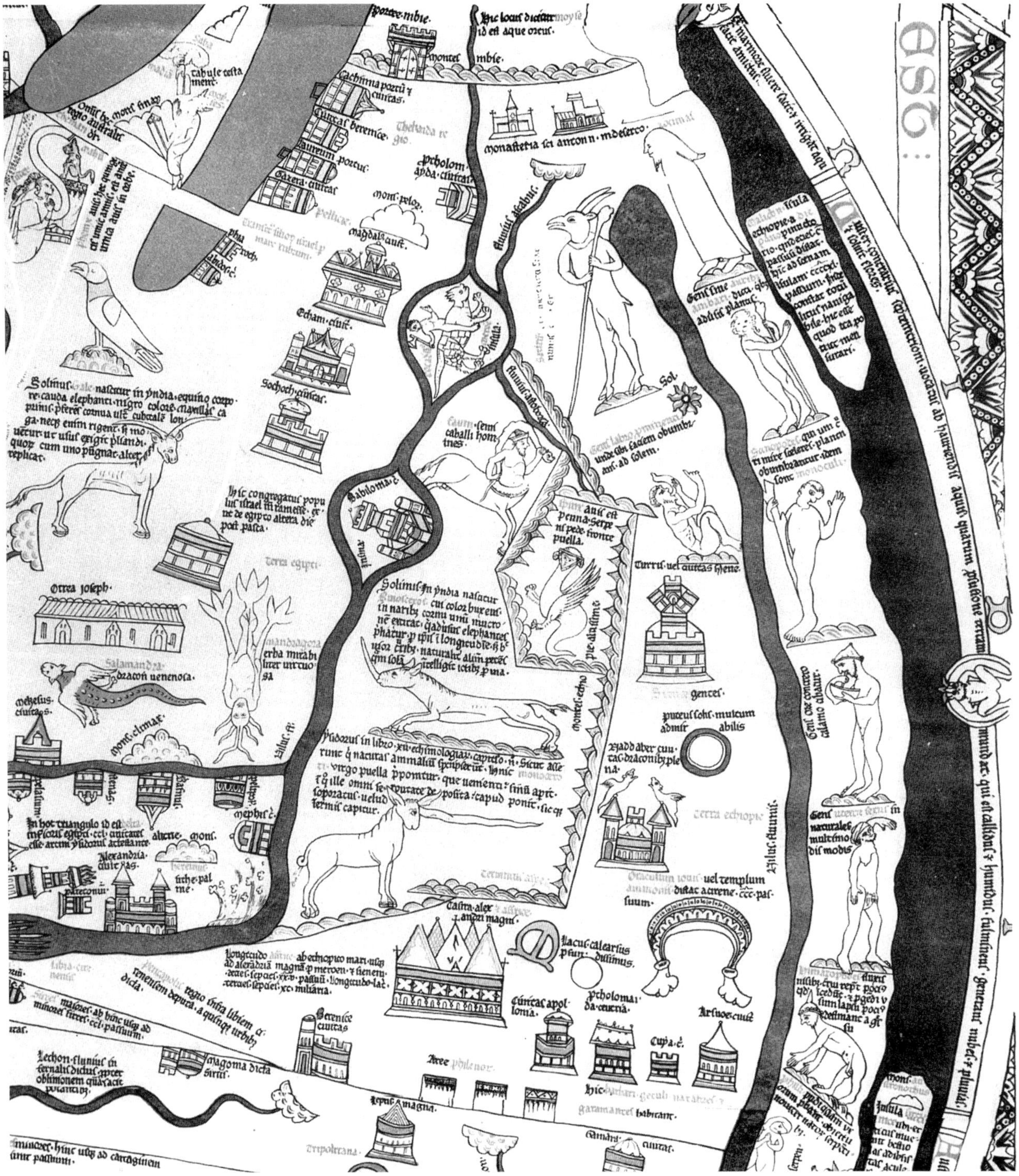

Section 6

SECTION 6

The river Nile leaves the mountains to flow through regions associated with the desert fathers of the third and fourth centuries and passes near the monastery of St. Anthony with its two delightful churches. A little below this a strange creature, hoofed, horned and bird-headed, may represent one of the beasts who troubled the saint.[1] The river divides to form two islands, one containing a crocodile bestridden by a man, the other a fine city denoting Cairo, and then forms its delta. Many settlements crowd the coast-line, among them Alexandria with its pharos.[2] To the left, the land of Egypt is filled with marvels, the mandrake, the salamander, the yale,[3] and the phoenix. Alongside these are references to Old Testament history. Joseph's barns, where the corn was stored in the years of plenty, are depicted as a large building in the style we know from ancient tithe-barns. Rameses is marked as the gathering place of the Israelites. The track of their journey to the Promised Land drives on through the Red Sea whose waters are parted for their passage. On its other side Moses receives the tables of the covenant.[4] Near at hand, the Israelites worship the golden calf. To the right hand of the river further strange creatures occupy a tract enclosed by mountains, among them a unicorn, the rhinoceros, the sphinx with its feet of a serpent, wings of a bird and face of a young woman.

Between the broad stream of the upper Nile and the encircling ocean is a kind of frieze of strange beings whose location indicates places beyond the limits of ordinary experience. They include people with no ears but with twisted feet, and others with mouths so made that they can take nourishment only through reeds.[5]

West of the mountains among which the unicorn is found is the boundary of Asia which includes Egypt. Africa begins here.

(1) St. Anthony retired into the desert c. 285 where he was reputed to fight with demons in the guise of beasts. Disciples were attracted to his holy life, and he organised them in a loose-knit community of hermits. See *The Sayings of the Desert Fathers*, trans. Benedicta Ward, Mowbray, 1975.

(2) The lighthouse on the island of Pharos outside Alexandria's Harbour was one of the wonders of the ancient world.

(3) Now thought to be the Indian water-buffalo. See Malcolm Letts, *The Pictures in the Hereford Mappa Mundi*, reprinted from *Notes and Queries*, Jan. 1955 in *The World Map in Hereford Cathedral*, by Prebendary A. L. Moir, 1970.

(4) Moses is shown, as so often in art, with horns, probably on account of a traditional confusion between 'cornutus' shining, and the word 'cornu', horn.

(5) Much of the lore concerning these strange creatures is ultimately derived from the writings of the elder Pliny, where the context is often India and the east.

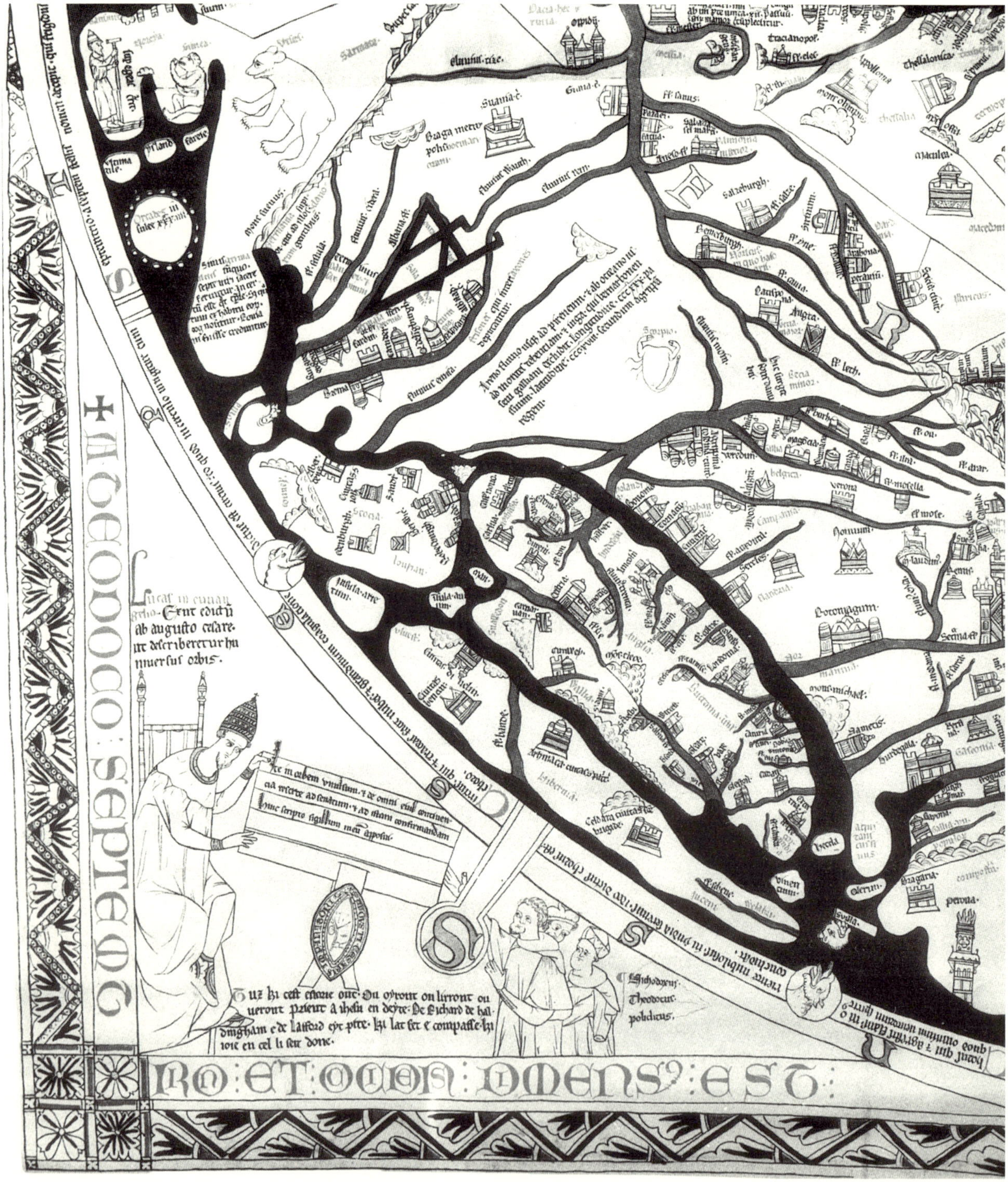
Lucas in euuangelio · Exiit edictum ab augusto cesare ut describeretur huniuersus orbis.
Tuz ki cest estoire ont · Ou oyront ou liront ou ueront prient a ihesu en deyte · De Richard de haldingham e de Lafford eyt pite · Ki lat fet e compassé · Ki ioie en cel li seit done.

Section 7

SECTION 7

The curve of the map towards the west has distorted the northern and western shores of Europe to an extent that makes their features difficult to recognise. At the top is Norway, marked with a tiny figure apparently wearing skis. A great bear places us firmly in regions east of the Vistula, and thence we can follow the coast along the Baltic Sea, past the rivers of North Germany, the Rhine and then the Seine. The peninsular thrust of Brittany has been smoothed away, but Mont St. Michele is prominently shown. The French Atlantic coast of Aquitaine is easier to recognise. The rivers which flow eastwards from the Rhine are those of the Danubian systems, draining to the Black Sea.

The British Isles are equally distorted, so that it would seem that what we think of as the Kentish coast lies opposite to Aquitaine. They lie on the outermost edge of the world. It is fortunate they are within the world's rim at all, for geography based on classical and early Christian thought placed them apart from Europe.[1]

Great Britain is divided into Scotland, Wales, England and Cornwall. Ireland, much elongated, lies alongside. The division of England from Wales by the rivers Dee and Severn and from Scotland by the Tweed must surely represent the boundary rather than indicate the actual course of the rivers, though in many cases the river systems, particularly of the north of England, are well shown. Snowdon fills North Wales as the Grampian mountains do the north of Scotland. A considerable number of towns are shown, notably in Ireland Kildare and Armagh, in Scotland St. Andrews and in Wales St. Davids, Conway and Caernarvon. In England, Lincoln stands on an eminence above the river Witham, Ely on an island apparently in the river Nene.[2] Hereford is poorly represented.

Other islands round the British seas are drawn. It seems likely that the monster labelled *Svilla* to the far west of Great Britain represents the Scilly Isles, a not inappropriate borrowing of monster, and, by false etymology, of name, from the Sicilian seas and depicted there.[3]

(1) R. W. Southern, *Medieval Humanism*, Cap III, quoting the description of Britain as an 'insula interfuso mari toto orbe divisa'. Isidore (c 560-636) whose *Etymologiae* was an encyclopedia of the knowledge of his time and source for much information given in this map.

(2) This seems strange. The Ouse is not identifiable.

(3) See Section 8.

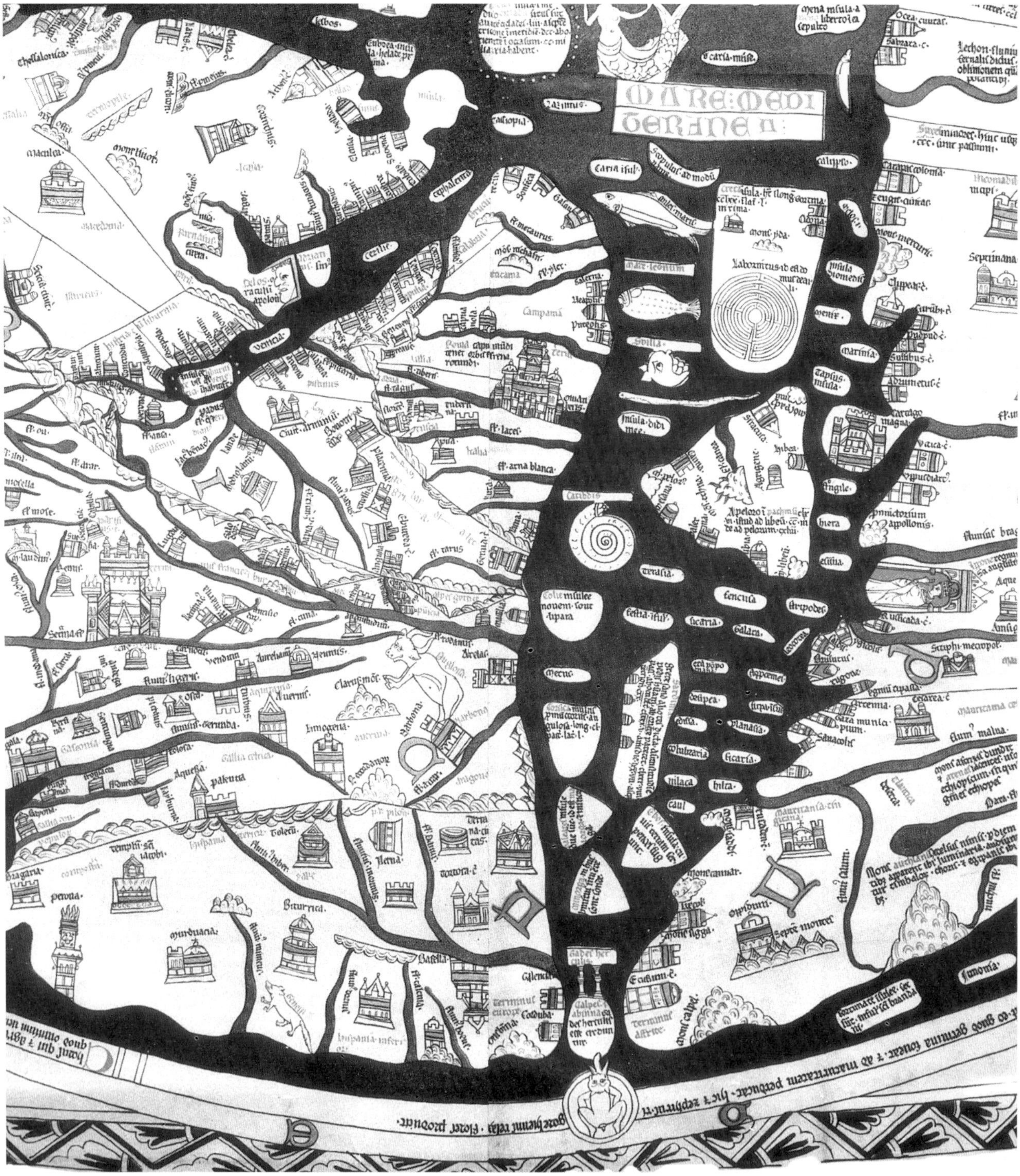

Section 8

SECTION 8

The western limits of the Mediterranean sea are marked by the Pillars of Hercules depicted as two columns on the island of Gades.[1] The outer seas to which the straits give access are filled, to the right, with islands, the first of them marked as the Fortunate Islands associated with St. Brendan.[2] Africa ends at the right of the straits. Its northern shore is rimmed with towns, many of which can be identified from the Antonine itineraries.[3] St. Augustine, robed, within a canopy, presides over Hippo. Carthage is a splendid city a little further up the coast.

From the west to east the Mediterranean is crammed with islands. The Balearics lie first. The inhabitants of Minorca are described as famous for their skill with the sling. Sardinia is shaped like a foot, Sicily is a large triangle with Etna spouting flames. Crete is dominated by its labyrinth.

Between Sicily and Italy, the straits are guarded by the whirlpool Charybdis and the monster Scylla (*Svilla*).[4]

On the left, the northern shore of the Mediterranean is bordered first by Spain, and then by southern France. Then Italy thrusts a blunted shape between the Mediterranean and Adriatic seas. The peninsular shape of Spain is destroyed by the distortion caused by the curve of the map. St. James' shrine at Compostella in northern Spain is marked.[5] The Pyrenees divide Spain from France where, in the south, a large bull is rather oddly labelled *Buglossa*. In Italy, Rome, who holds the reins of the world, is pre-eminent, in France, Paris is splendidly betowered on the banks of the Seine.[6] Venice is shown as an island in the Adriatic.[7] Beyond this sea, Greece appears surprisingly empty. The location of places famous in story and by association seems sometimes confused. Delphi, for example, seems to have been mixed with Delos.

(1) This demonstrates some confusion. Gades is Cadiz. The legend of Hercules tells that the hero tore a passage between Europe and Africa to reach Gades. It was supposed that columns were later set on either side as seamarks. Brewer's *Dictionary of phrase and fable*.

(2) Probably to be identified with Madeira and the Canaries group. St. Brendan was an Irish saint of the fifth century. His voyages were first recounted in the ninth century. The search for blest isles becomes a spiritual pilgrimage. *Lives of the Saints* (Penguin Classics).

(3) The Antonine Itineraries are a compilation of information about routes needful for troop movements through the Roman Empire. They date from the third century. A.D.

(4) Charybdis' whirlpool is strangely shaped like an ammonite. The monster Svilla reappears in the seas south of the British Isles. See Section 7.

(5) Compostella was, after the Holy Land, the most important centre of medieval pilgrimage. T. D. Kenerick *St. James in Spain* (1960).

(6) At sometime unknown, an attempt seems to have been made to deface Paris on the map.

(7) Venice was perhaps at this time even more familiar as the embarcation port for pilgrimages to the Holy Land than as a trading centre.

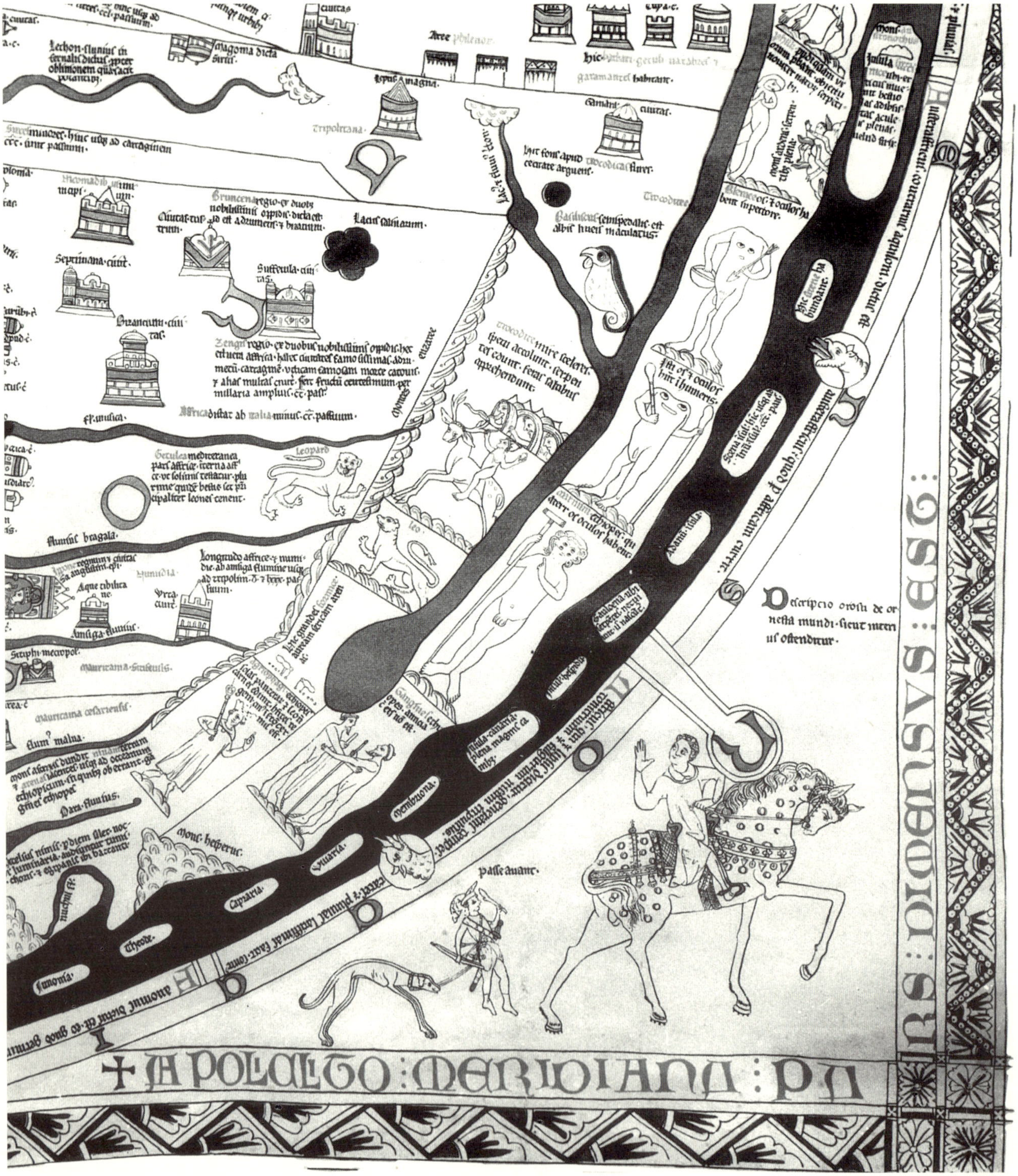

Section 9

SECTION 9

The map is relatively empty for the areas of Africa inland from the Mediterranean coast. There are few historical associations and it is difficult not to see the few towns mentioned as rather randomly set down. A range of mountains, which we would know as Atlas, runs at an angle to divide the northward-looking lands of the Roman Empire from the interior. An heraldic-looking leopard waves its tail. In the fastnesses of the mountains we are given a lion, and a little above him, the Troglodytes are living in their caves, eating serpents, and catching wild animals by riding on their backs. Near them is a strange bird-like creature, the basilisk.[1] Beneath the lion are gold-digging ants,[2] and below them again the one-eyed king of Ethiopians who eat only the flesh of panthers and lions.

Beyond the upper Nile the frieze of strange creatures continues, among them the Pyslli exhibiting their young to red-tongued serpents,[3] the Blemyes and Antropophagi whose heads are beneath their shoulders, and the race with such keen sight that they are depicted with four eyes.

The outer sea is filled with Islands. Opposite the four-eyed figure is Grand Canary. It carries an inscription that it is full of large dogs, an example of images determined by false etymology.

(1) The basilisk, usually thought of as a serpent hatched from a cock's egg (cockatrice) is sometimes depicted as half-bird, half-serpent, as here, or, for example, on the west front of Amiens cathedral. Its glance dealt death.

(2) Stories of gold-digging ants as big as foxes or wolves are told by Herodotus and repeated by Pliny. In the heat of the day while the ants slept, men could steal the gold they had dug.

(3) These must be the people who, according to Pliny, made a gainful trade of bringing into Italy poisons of other countries, and filled Italy with venomous beasts (Pliny's *Natural History*, Philemon Holland's translation, 1601). This probably refers to what had been a trade in medicines.

Beyond the rim of the curved world, the horseman rides away. We have looked at the map of the world. Let us examine the world of the map.

THE WORLD OF THE MAP

The illustrations in this booklet have been taken from the lithograph made from drawings and published in 1869 through the initiative of Prebendary F.T. Havergal, to whose informed enthusiasm the cathedral of Hereford owed, and still owes, a great debt. For nearly a hundred years this was the only available full-scale copy of the map. Shortly after the 1939-45 war the Royal Geographical Society generously met the cost of restoration work and at that time made a photographic facsimile copy. This was published in the Society's series of *Reproductions of Early Manuscript Maps,* as number III, in 1954. The photographs, however, are not as clear in further reproduction as the old lithograph version. The sections into which the map has been divided for the purpose of this booklet largely correspond to those of the 1954 publication. This means that the descriptions can be used alongside the photographic facsimile by those who have access to this now rare and expensive work.

The only full-scale book devoted to the map was published in 1873. This, too, is now difficult to obtain. It was written by the Rev. W. L. Bevan, vicar of Hay, a considerable historical geographer, and the Rev. H. W. Phillott, rector of Staunton-on-Wye, a classical scholar.[1] The map needs these two disciplines hand-in-hand for its exposition. This book has not been superseded in its provision of a transcription of most of the text, with careful notes on the sources, combined with a geographical description. The Royal Geographical Society's publication of 1954 was accompanied by a memoir written by Mr. G.R. Crone, who there and in further work did much to make clear the antiquity of the map's cartographical form and geographical content while demonstrating that it does, particularly in the selection of towns given in Western Europe, make some contribution to thirteenth century geography. Mr. Crone has shown that this choice may indicate a knowledge of, and wish to illustrate, certain trade and pilgrim routes.[2] Scholars in other fields have turned to a study of this map for its inconographical significance and for what it reveals of the intellectual world of its time.

This little booklet leans heavily on the work of others. It is provided to replace the guide prepared by Prebendary A. L. Moir for visitors to the Cathedral.[3] This prompted much interest in the map, particularly in the field of its religious significance, but has long been out of print and could not be reproduced because of difficulties with the illustrations.

(1) *Medieval Geography, An Essay in illustration of the Hereford Mappa Mundi,* The Rev. W. L. Bevan and the Rev. H. W. Phillott 1873. The Rev. H. W. Phillott was a canon of Hereford Cathedral and a generous benefactor to it.

(2) *Reproductions of Medieval Maps,* op. cit. The road to Compostella from France to Spain for example is probably indicated by the choice of a town like Jaca, south of the Pyrenees, otherwise an unremarkable place.

(3) *The World Map in Hereford Cathedral,* Prebendary A. L. Moir.

It is generally accepted that in cartographical form and, for the most part, in geographical content, the Hereford map is of considerable antiquity. Adherence to tradition and convention has forced the map into distortions in scale and outline which are likely to mislead us at a first encounter. It would be naive indeed to assume that this map provides us with a statement of all that the thirteenth century knew of space and distance. A world which had experience of the journeyings of the Crusaders, of pilgrimages as far as Jerusalem, constant and continuing contact with Rome and with centres of learning, trade by land and sea, would have more awareness, for example, of the relative distance between places than this map can represent. Any man going on a journey in any age can calculate distance by the time it takes to cover it. We are left pondering on the extent to which such a map would have been of practical guidance. Richard de Haldingham and Lafford asks for the prayers of all who should read or see or hear his map. This last seems important. It would be possible for a group of intending travellers to have read out to them, at any rate for Western Europe and the Mediterranean basin, a list, in due order, of towns to be passed through on a journey to a given destination. The traveller could learn the name of the next place to be asked for. He is provided, in fact, with a rough itinerary.

To provide an itinerary is one of the functions of a map, but not necessarily its first purpose. The itinerary is a bye-product. The dictionary definition of a map is 'a plane figure representing the surface of the earth or part of it'. The Hereford map is just this, and therefore does what all maps are designed to do, shows places in relation to each other. Distances and shapes may be distorted, but even so, by an imaginative grasp that is astonishing, the four quarters of the world are represented. We are shown, for example, Constantinople on the Black Sea in relation to the mountains of Armenia, through which, by the Caspian Gates, is the passage to central Asia and the illimitable distances of the East. Illimitable distance in a few inches square is no mean achievement.

The almost total reliance on geographical knowledge unrevised for 1000 years has not prevented the Hereford map from being reckoned with as a map, but this is not its essential remarkable quality. That lies in the way in which a totality of information, again culled mostly from ancient book-learning, has been presented within the terms and form of a map to provide what is at once a statement about, and a celebration of, the world and its marvels. It is in this that the map is for us today a guide to its own time. It provides a particularly vivid light both on the images and associations with which men's minds were filled, and to some extent on how those images came to be formed.

The sources of the descriptions given alongside the symbols and drawings have in many cases been charted in the work of Bevan and Phillott.

The Bible of course, particularly the Old Testament, is richly in evidence. Much seems to be taken from the writings of Solinus which were in turn based on the elder Pliny's *Natural History*. A good deal goes back on Orosius and Isidore.

Classical writings, from Herodotus onwards, are the base for the information found in medieval bestiaries popular from the twelfth century, and Pliny again is the main source of tales for Alexander popularised in French, and later English verse stories which were possibly available to the compilers of these maps.[4]

Much work needs to be done on the use made of these sources, and questions are to be asked and answered concerning the choice of such material, the influence of its availability on thought, and the versions which were referred to. The thirteenth century was almost obsessive in its compilation of encyclopedias of knowledge. It is possible that it is from compilation made from compilation that the map-makers took their information but that in the urge to claim authority a more direct quotation is given than is strictly true. This would explain some of the many mistakes and rather garbled versions expounded by Bevan and Phillott. It is likely that not all these errors can be explained as scribal mistakes.

However obtained, and at whatever number of removes from its original source, the information supplied was current in the thirteenth century. It was the stuff of general knowledge, the common culture of a civilisation, and it is manifested in many contexts. Emile Male[5] says 'It is . . . as a mappa mundi that we should interpret the famous doorway at Vézelay', and describes the carvings of Sens cathedral among which the elephant, the treasure-guarding griffin, the Sciapod, are all included. In his book he discusses the encyclopedic work of Vincent of Beauvais (died 1264) called *Speculum Majus* which was intended to be a compendium of the whole range of knowledge, a *Mirror* of the world and a statement of God's plan for it. He then illustrates how these ideas and this accumulated knowledge can be traced in the facades of thirteenth century cathedrals in France. Our Hereford map in its curious combination of text, drawing and cartography also provides an illustration of the passage to and fro of knowledge and ideas until they become common coinage and fixed by usage.

This brings us back to the map and to a better understanding of its value to its times. If the common culture of the day was aware of the elephant and the rhinoceros, knew its Old Testament history, had heard of the wonders of the ancient world, was familiar with the stories of Alexander's heroic campaigns, then a map which showed these things in their place, marked their location, would be a marvel. It would complete the imaginative hold on the material.

(4) Solinus, writing after AD200 compiled *Collectanea Rerum Memorabilium* 'Almost the whole is taken from Pliny's Natural History and Mela [writing in 37-41 AD] without acknowledgement' (Oxford Classical Dictionary). Pliny's *Natural History* is available in the Loeb edition. For Orosius see p 3, and for Isidore, see p. 21. An English version of the Alexander Romance, entitled *King Alisaunder* is published by the Early English Text Society, ed. G. V. Smithers, 1952.

(5) op. cit. p. 4.

If, on the other hand, the interest and purpose of the map is primarily geographical, and the fixing of the place more important than its association (that is the content illustrates the map, not the map the content), then the choice made of illustration, of the association to be marked, becomes of profound interest in showing us something of the furniture of men's minds 700 years ago. In some respects we reach back to them. Colchis still conjures the golden fleece, India can still be symbolised by the elephant, but in others we are a long way off. Rhodes does not mean the Colossus, and Crete is the Palace of Minos for we know too much now about the labyrinth.

The Sciapod we dismiss as some half-understood monkey. We are probably nearer to the thirteenth century in thinking of fabulous creatures when we ponder on the Loch Ness monster or the Yeti. The Holy Land is not the centre of the world but a tiny tract of country between east and west.

The map is astonishingly full of detail. Much has had to be passed over within the scope of this booklet, but one thing must strike those who look at it with care. Everything is going on at once. The map may be concerned with space, but time is encapsulated. One is reminded of pictures in Books of Hours of a slightly later date, where the Magi are seen at once coming over the hills and also arrived at Bethlehem. It is easy to dismiss this as a naiveté, but this would be a wrong judgement. The map is providing a whole statement about the world planned by God. In this, everything is caught up and held, past and present, near and far.

It is thought that the map was completed in about the year 1290. It comes at the end of a phase in fashion in learning, but in many ways it is a precursor of times to come. A map like this was preparing the ground for an educated laity which, in about 80 years, was to be reading Chaucer.[6]

(6) See *English Friars and antiquity*, Beryl Smalley, Blackwell, 1960. In Chapter I she discusses the growth of a lay reading public in the early fourteenth century, the matter that was appealing to it, and the stories that were relished. Much of it is the kind of material appearing in this map.